FASCINATING FACTS
ABOUT HAWAI‘I

DID YOU KNOW?

Hawai'i was the first state to ban non-compostable
plastic bags at checkout counters.

———————————

In the Islands, a mixed-breed mutt is
called a poi dog.

———————————

The first California-Hawai'i flight made a
forced landing at sea—then floated the rest of the way
with a rigged sail.

———————————

There are no seagulls in Hawai'i.

FASCINATING FACTS

—ABOUT—

HAWAI'I

by Jim Loomis

WATERMARK
PUBLISHING

ISBN 978-1-948011

Library of Congress Control Number: 2019933375

Design and production   Kristin Lipman
Editor   George Engebretson

Watermark Publishing
1000 Bishop St., Ste. 806
Honolulu, HI 96813
Toll-free 1-866-900-BOOK
sales@bookshawaii.net
www.bookshawaii.net

PRINTED IN KOREA

FAST FACT

Honolulu's Our Lady of Peace is the oldest Catholic cathedral in continuous use in the US.

Contents

INTRODUCTION

I wasn't very far into this project when an uncomfortable truth became apparent: A book called *Fascinating Facts About Hawai'i* will never be "complete" because there are literally hundreds of things—from quirky trivia to world-shaking events—that I find fascinating even after living in Hawai'i for more than 50 years.

Some of these facts may be of only passing interest to you. Still, in my travels across the country and around the world, I've found that most people are very interested in hearing about Hawai'i, and are truly fascinated by the many things that are unique to these incomparable islands.

Every reasonable effort has been made to confirm the accuracy of all names and dates, and I apologize in advance for any discrepancies that may appear in these pages.

JIM LOOMIS
Ha'ikū, Maui

FAST FACT

In August 2018, lava flowing from Kīlauea added 900 acres to the Big Island coastline.

ISLANDS

KAUA'I

NI'IHAU

O'AHU

There are more than 120 Hawaiian islands.

A map of Hawai'i typically shows eight islands, and indeed there are eight major islands in the chain. From west to east: Ni'ihau, Kaua'i, O'ahu, Moloka'i, Lāna'i, Kaho'olawe, Maui and Hawai'i. But here are also scores of islets, reefs and shoals—extending on a diagonal from Hawai'i island in the southeast to Kure Atoll, more than 1,500 miles away to the northwest. There are more than 120 of these islands, which together comprise the state of Hawai'i.

MOLOKA'I

MAUI

LĀNA'I

KAHO'OLAWE

HAWAI'I

HAWAI'I IS THE MOST ISOLATED POPULATED SPOT ON EARTH.

In the Aloha State, you're a long way from anywhere, even when traveling by jet. From Honolulu, it's 2,563 miles to Los Angeles, 2,398 to San Francisco and 2,683 to Seattle. Distances from Honolulu to other destinations around the Pacific:

Tokyo 3,860

Beijing 5,075

Sydney 5,080

Manila 5,300

Tahiti 2,757

Samoa 2,611

Guam 3,800

HAWAI'I ISN'T FOR EVERYONE.

Not everyone is comfortable living in such isolation. Some local businesses are even reluctant to hire new arrivals, who might come down with "rock fever" and move on after a few months.

HAWAI'I RUNS ON STANDARD TIME YEAR-ROUND.

In summer Honolulu is six hours behind Boston, five hours behind Chicago, four hours behind Denver and three hours behind Los Angeles. Subtract an hour from those numbers in winter, when the rest of the country switches from daylight savings time back to standard time—but Hawai'i stays put.

ALL THAT GLITTERS ARE NOT
diamonds.

The extinct volcanic crater named Diamond Head on O'ahu was so named because 19th century British sailors thought they'd found diamonds on its slopes. Unfortunately for them, the "diamonds" were only calcite crystals, but the name stuck.

HONOLULU IS A BIG PLACE.

The City & County of Honolulu includes not only the island of O'ahu but all of the Northwestern Hawaiian Islands (those west of Ni'ihau) except Midway Atoll, making Honolulu the most far-flung county in the country.

HOW TO ASK FOR DIRECTIONS IN HONOLULU.

Don't expect north south, east or west. Instead you'll hear the words *mauka* (MAU-kuh), which means "toward the mountains" and *makai* (mah-KAI), "toward the ocean." And depending where you are in town, west is *'ewa* (toward the West O'ahu town of 'Ewa) and east is *diamondhead* or *kokohead*—in the direction of those two geological features.

HAWAI'I CAN CLAIM THE WETTEST SPOT ON EARTH.

It's on the island of Kaua'i at the 5,148-foot summit of Mount Wai'ale'ale, where rainfall averages about 450 inches a year. (That's more than 37 feet!)

FAST FACT

In January 2019 Waipā Gardens on Kaua'i set the US rainfall record with 50 inches in 24 hours.

WAI'ALE'ALE

ELEV 5148FT →

THE TALLEST MOUNTAIN IN THE WORLD IS ON THE ISLAND OF HAWAIʻI.

At 29,035 feet, Mount Everest is the world's highest mountain *above sea level*. Mauna Kea ("White Mountain") on the Island of Hawaiʻi rises 13,796 feet above sea level, but it also extends some 19,700 feet below the surface to the floor of the Pacific Ocean—for a total height of nearly 33,500 feet.

IT'S NOT THE FAR WEST, BUT THE DEEP SOUTH.

People commonly consider Hawai'i to be the westernmost state in the Union. The fact is, Alaska extends farther west. Hawai'i is the farthest south, however. Ka Lae (South Point) on the Big Island is the southernmost spot in the US.

IN HAWAI'I, YOU CAN WATER SKI AND SNOW SKI ON THE SAME DAY.

A few times each year, the Big Island's two 14,000-foot peaks, Mauna Loa and Mauna Kea, get enough snow for skiing. And if they were so inclined, skiers could kick off their skis and drive down to Kealakekua Bay to spend the rest of the day water skiing.

THIS BIG ISLAND VOLCANO HAS BEEN ERUPTING SINCE 1983.

These days, the state's only volcanic activity takes place on the island of Hawai'i, the largest island in the chain and, geologically speaking, the youngest. The active volcano of Kilauea has been erupting nonstop since 1983, sometimes in dramatic fashion as in 2018. Even when there are no towering fountains of lava, Kīlauea can generate as many as a hundred earthquakes a day. Most are deep underground and even the more severe temblors produce only a mild shaking. Stronger earthquakes do occur occasionally.

THE LARGEST DORMANT VOLCANO IN THE WORLD IS ON MAUI.

Haleakalā, or "House of the Sun," is 10,023 feet above sea level at its summit. The inside of the crater is about 7.5 miles long by 2.5 miles wide. Haleakalā is classified as dormant, which means that theoretically it can erupt at any time. Not to worry, though. Volcanologists have determined that Haleakalā hasn't erupted since the late 1700s.

WHY DON'T PEOPLE LIVE ON KAHO'OLAWE?

The island of Kaho'olawe lies seven miles off the south coast of Maui. With no mountains, the island has almost no water, yet several hundred Hawaiians lived there for many generations. Kaho'olawe is deserted today, and for good reason. Beginning in the 1930s, the island was used by the US military for practice bombing and shelling. While a case could be made for this during World War II, the bombing continued for years despite constant objections from the State of Hawai'i. The military finally ceased fire in 1990 and the island was returned to the State four years later. There have been several serious attempts to clean up the island and make it safe for visitors again, but there's still too much unexploded ordinance. Kaho'olawe will undoubtedly remain dangerous—and uninhabited—for years to come.

THERE'S ANOTHER ISLAND ON THE WAY.

Loʻihi is an underwater volcano—technically, that's called a seamount—located about 20 miles off the southeast coast of the Big Island. University of Hawaiʻi oceanographer Alex Malahoff and his assistant Terry Kerby explored the base of Loʻihi in a Russian submersible, descending to a depth of 16,750 feet, or 3.17 miles. Loʻihi is still almost 3,000 feet below sea level, and scientists estimate it won't break the surface for another 100,000 years.

WHY CAN'T I HOP A PLANE TO Niʻihau?

Lying to the west of Kauaʻi, Niʻihau is Hawaiʻi's private island. In 1864, King Kamehameha V sold it to Elizabeth Sinclair for $10,000 and the island is still owned by her descendants to this day. It's a small island—just 72 square miles compared to Oʻahu's 600—with a declining population estimated at fewer than 70 people, most of whom speak Hawaiian as their native language. A small Navy installation on the island provides a few jobs, while some islanders support themselves by subsistence fishing and farming.

FAST FACT

In 1929, the Ala Wai Canal drained Waikīkī's swamps, laying the foundation for all those hotels.

KALAWAO IS AMERICA'S SMALLEST COUNTY.

Located on Moloka'i's northern coast, Kalawao County on the Makanalua Peninsula is the smallest county in the US in both population and land area. It's the site of the Kalaupapa settlement for patients of Hansen's disease.

THERE ARE NO TOWN OR CITY GOVERNMENTS IN HAWAI'I.

In addition to the federal government, there are only two other levels of government in the Islands—county and state. Kaua'i, O'ahu and Hawai'i are all separate counties, each with its own elected mayor and city or county council. Maui County encompasses Maui, Moloka'i and Lāna'i. To make sure Moloka'i and Lāna'i folks aren't left out of the political process, county meetings are held on all three islands.

HONOLULU IS BIGGER THAN YOU THINK.

The City & County of Honolulu has a population of about one million people, more than San Francisco, Portland, Seattle, Denver, Omaha, St. Louis, Boston or Miami.

HONOLULU'S BUS SYSTEM IS ONE OF THE BEST.

Dubbed simply TheBus, it has twice been recognized by the American Public Transportation Association as "America's Best Transit System."

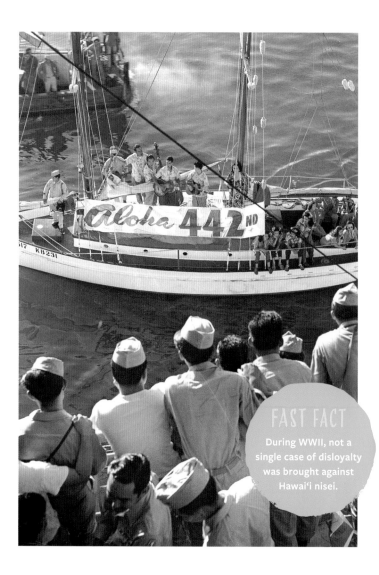

chapter 2

HISTORY

Maybe Captain Cook wasn't the first westerner to discover Hawai'i.

While the noted English explorer Captain James Cook usually gets credit for discovering the Hawaiian Islands for the western world in 1778 (death on the Big Island, opposite), there is also evidence that the very first westerners were Spanish sailors, who made regular crossings between Mexico and the Philippines in the 16th and 17th centuries.

HAWAI'I'S FIRST *REAL* DISCOVERERS.

But the very first humans to set foot in the Islands were Polynesian navigators from the Marquesas and Tahiti, who arrived some 1,000 years ago. These intrepid sailors crossed almost 2,000 miles of open ocean in large double-hulled voyaging canoes. It was an incredible feat of seamanship— once they crossed the equator into the northern hemisphere, the stars by which they navigated were largely new and different. Once the new islands were populated, these ancient mariners sailed back and forth between north and south.

Seven Kings and a Queen

KAMEHAMEHA I *(1795-1819)*

The first of all the Hawaiian kings (opposite). In the late 1700s, he raised and launched an army from his home on the Big Island, quickly overcoming defending armies on Maui and Moloka'i. By 1800, all the islands of Hawai'i were united under his rule.

KAMEHAMEHA II *(1819-1824)*

Abolished the *kapu* (taboo) system, which had ruled the daily lives of every Hawaiian, and died of pneumonia while on a state visit to England.

KAMEHAMEHA III *(1825-1854)*

Reigned for 25 years, the longest of any Hawaiian monarch. He welcomed the first Protestant missionaries, oversaw the creation of a constitution for Hawai'i and introduced the Great Māhele, which for the first time let both native Hawaiians and foreigners own land in Hawai'i.

KAMEHAMEHA IV *(1855-1863)*

Bitterly opposed an early effort led by American businessmen and missionaries to see Hawai'i annexed by the United States.

KAMEHAMEHA V *(1863-1872)*

Wrote a constitution that remained in effect for almost 25 years. He weighed 375 pounds when he died of morbid obesity, ending the Kamehameha dynasty.

LUNALILO *(1873-1874)*

First Hawaiian monarch elected by the Hawaiian legislature. He used his powers to amend the constitution, eliminating the provision that only property owners were eligible to vote.

KALĀKAUA *(1874-1891)*

The "Merrie Monarch" encouraged all forms of traditional Hawaiian entertainment, including the previously banned hula.

LILIʻUOKALANI *(1891-1893)*

To avoid bloodshed, the first and only woman to serve as head of state reluctantly agreed to her kingdom's takeover by US-backed forces, which established the short-lived Republic of Hawaiʻi. While under house arrest at ʻIolani Palace, she wrote *Aloha ʻOe (Farewell to You)*, one of the best known and most loved of all Hawaiian songs.

HAWAI'I WAS A CONSTITUTIONAL MONARCHY.

At the time of its annexation, and after almost 100 years as a traditional hereditary monarchy, Hawai'i adopted a constitution that called for its kings and queens to be elected by popular vote.

READY OR NOT, HAWAI'I JOINS THE UNITED STATES.

In the late 1800s, economic ties between the Kingdom of Hawai'i and the US were growing stronger, as American businessmen dominated both Island politics and the Hawaiian economy. In 1893 Queen Lili'uokalani's efforts to strengthen the monarchy prompted business leaders to depose her in a bloodless coup and, the following year, send a delegation to Washington in an unsuccessful move to secure American annexation. In 1896, William McKinley was elected president and the annexation was signed a year after that.

ONE MAN'S ANNEXATION IS ANOTHER MAN'S OVERTHROW.

One reason Hawai'i was annexed in the face of strong local opposition was that Spain had colonized Puerto Rico and the Philippines, and the US government worried that Hawai'i might be next. The main attraction for the US and several other powers was Pearl Harbor and its strategic military importance as a large, safe harbor offering sanctuary for ships in the middle of the vast Pacific Ocean.

CALL IT HANSEN'S DISEASE.

Kalaupapa is a 16-square-mile peninsula on the north side of Moloka'i where sufferers of leprosy—now called Hansen's disease— were exiled beginning in the 1860s. At one time, some 1,200 people called Kalaupapa home; today only a handful live there by choice. (Hansen's disease has been under control since the advent of sulfone drugs in the late 1940s.) Kalaupapa is accessible by plane or by a breathtaking mule ride traversing the face of the world's tallest sea cliffs—a sheer drop of more than 2,000 feet down to the sea from the upcountry area Moloka'i residents call "topside."

THE DAY GEORGE PATTON BOMBED MAUNA LOA.

The year was 1935 and the sprawling Big Island volcano was erupting, threatening several homes. So General George S. Patton, stationed in Hawai'i at the time, ordered an air strike on Mauna Loa. Several World War I vintage bombers flew to the Big Island the day after Christmas and dropped their bombs on the river of hot lava. Two days later, the lava flow slowed, then stopped altogether.

Hawai'i is home to the only royal palace in the United States.

'Iolani Palace in downtown Honolulu was built during the reign of King Kalākaua. Construction was completed in 1882 and the building served as the official residence of Hawaiian royalty until 1893, when the Hawaiian monarchy was toppled.

AND THEN THERE WAS *light*

King Kalākaua had great interest in technology and even got a quick lesson in how a light bulb works from Thomas Edison himself. In 1887, Princess Kaʻiulani flipped a switch in ʻIolani Palace and the royal residence was illuminated with electric lighting. The White House in Washington didn't have electric lights until 1889.

THE LURE OF A PLANTATION PAYDAY.

There were very few Chinese in Hawaiʻi until 1852, when 175 contract workers from Hong Kong arrived on Maui to work on the sugar plantations. They were paid $3 a month plus room and board. Their numbers grew substantially, with many leaving plantation work and opening mercantile shops instead. In the ensuing years they were replaced in the cane and pineapple fields by new contract workers imported from Japan, Portugal, Korea, the Philippines, Puerto Rico and the South Pacific.

Hawai'i at War

GO FOR BROKE

FAST FACT

Nimble-fingered lei sellers were pressed into duty to weave camouflage nets.

THERE WERE *TWO* ATTACKS ON PEARL HARBOR.
Everyone knows about the Japanese attack on December 7, 1941, but almost no one remembers that there was a second attack by a pair of Japanese seaplanes. The two planes carried a bomb under each wing and flew 2,000 miles from the Marshall Islands, arriving over Oʻahu in the early morning hours of March 2, 1942. Because the pilot of the lead plane became disoriented, all four bombs were dropped into Honolulu's Makiki neighborhood, several miles from Pearl Harbor. No one was hurt, but fears of more attacks persisted for months afterward.

CLOSE CALL FOR A COMMERCIAL AIRLINER ON DECEMBER 7.
On the morning of the Japanese attack on Pearl Harbor, a Hawaiian Airlines passenger plane was being prepped for a regularly scheduled inter-island flight. One of the attacking Japanese Zero fighters dove on the sitting duck and cut loose with its machine guns. The bad news: Several bullets struck the Hawaiian Airlines plane, starting a fire in the cockpit. The good news: A second Zero swooped in right behind the first and fired another round of bullets—one of which struck and activated the plane's automatic fire extinguisher, putting out the fire. This Hawaiian Air plane continued to fly passengers throughout the Islands until long after the end of the war.

AMERICA'S FIRST JAPANESE PRISONER OF WAR WAS CAPTURED ON NI'IHAU.

He was 22-year-old Airman 1st Class Shigenori Nishikaichi, whose plane was damaged during the raid on Pearl Harbor. Nishikaichi crash-landed on the remote island of Ni'ihau. The Hawaiians there had no idea that Pearl Harbor had been attacked and Nishikaichi was treated as a guest. But after a few days, the news finally reached the remote little island and the pilot was taken prisoner. After several hours in captivity, Nishikaichi escaped, only to be caught and killed in a fight with one of his captors.

THE MOST DECORATED UNIT IN THE HISTORY OF THE US ARMY.

In late 1942, the Army announced the formation of the 100th Infantry Battalion, to be made up of Americans of Japanese ancestry. In Hawai'i, 10,000 young men immediately volunteered and some 2,700 of them were accepted and sent to Camp Shelby, Mississippi, for basic training. Several months later, the Army created a second unit: the 442nd Regimental Combat Team. Like the 100th Battalion, the 442nd was manned almost entirely by young Japanese Americans, nearly all of them volunteers from Hawai'i. (The Army also insisted that all the unit's officers must be Caucasian.) After basic training, most of these new

recruits were shipped off to Italy, where they were rushed into combat and took heavy casualties.

They were then ordered to France to join the heavy fighting in the Vosges Mountains, where a Texas battalion had been cut off and trapped in a heavily forested area. The 442nd was sent in to rescue them. It took them five days, but the soldiers from Hawai'i broke through the German lines and led 211 Texas boys to safety. It came at an awful cost to the 442nd, with more than 800 young men killed or wounded. In total, 21 of these Hawai'i soldiers were awarded Congressional Medals of Honor for their extraordinary valor—this in addition to 52 Distinguished Service Crosses, 588 Silver Stars, 9,500 Purple Hearts, 5,200 Bronze Stars and seven Distinguished Unit Citations. And all of this while thousands of Japanese Americans, including many of the soldiers' friends and relatives, were held involuntarily in internment camps and relocation centers around the country.

THE LEGACY OF THE 442ND.

After the war, veterans of the 442nd and 100th Battalion returned home, earned college degrees under the GI Bill and became leaders in business and politics, including US Senators Spark Matsunaga and Daniel K. Inouye, both now deceased. Inouye, who lost his right arm while fighting in Italy, served for 50 years in the Senate, where he earned national acclaim during the Watergate hearings. Today, Honolulu's international airport (HNL) is named for him.

HAWAI'I LIVED UNDER MARTIAL LAW FOR ALMOST THE ENTIRE WAR.

During this time, the Islands' civilian population enjoyed few of the basic rights afforded other American citizens. Some four hundred people were arrested and jailed immediately after the attack on Pearl Harbor, as authorities clamped down on Hawai'i's Japanese community: Buddhist temples were summarily closed. Japanese language schools were shut down and their principals and many of their teachers arrested. The entire community faced a 6:00 p.m. curfew, large gatherings were forbidden, and food and fuel were rationed. Martial law remained in effect in Hawai'i until October of 1944, less than a year before the war ended.

HAWAI'I'S ETHNIC JAPANESE POPULATION PAID A HEAVY PRICE.

In a matter of hours after the bombing of Pearl Harbor, life became difficult indeed for residents of Japanese ancestry. Japanese-American members of the Hawai'i National Guard had their weapons confiscated. Thousands of young men in Hawai'i tried to enlist in the military but were rejected because most were *nisei* — sons of parents born in Japan. Almost anyone of Japanese ancestry was reclassified 4-C—Enemy Alien.

WHY WEREN'T HAWAI'I'S JAPANESE AMERICANS SENT TO INTERNMENT CAMPS?

While some 1,700 community leaders were interned on the mainland, most Japanese in the Islands were spared exile to relocation camps, largely out of economic necessity. As the Territory's biggest ethnic group, they were the backbone of the local labor force, particularly on the plantations, and were also critical to the war effort in tasks such as the building of defenses. Japanese Americans were also tightly woven into Hawai'i's cultural fabric, and authorities recognized that their removal would have a devastating effect on morale island-wide.

THE BOOKENDS OF
PEARL HARBOR

That's the informal name given to the two US Navy
battleships now at rest at Pearl Harbor. The *USS Arizona*
was sunk on December 7, a symbol of the beginning of
WWII, now lying beneath the Arizona Memorial with
more than 1,000 sailors still entombed inside. Nearby is
the battleship *USS Missouri*, on whose deck the treaty
ending the war was signed in Tokyo Bay.

The changing face of Hawai'i politics

The end of World War II brought a tidal wave of change to Hawai'i politics, as more and more "locals" (usually meaning non-white Island residents)—now more worldly and better educated—ran for office and won influential positions in the decades that followed. (Before the war, local business and government had been dominated mostly by the descendants of American missionaries, sugar planters and merchants.) Among this new breed of Hawai'i government leaders:

HIRAM FONG

first Asian American elected to the US Senate

DANIEL INOUYE

first Japanese American elected to the US House of Representatives and the first elected to the US Senate

---

PATSY MINK

first Asian-American woman elected to Congress

DANIEL AKAKA

first Native Hawaiian elected to Congress

GEORGE ARIYOSHI

first Japanese American elected governor of a state

JOHN WAIHEE

first Native Hawaiian elected governor of a state

BEN CAYETANO

first Filipino American elected governor of a state

TULSI GABBARD

first Samoan American elected to Congress

BARACK OBAMA

first African American elected US president

PATSY MINK, TITLE IX PIONEER.

While serving in the US House, Hawai'i's Patsy Mink authored the Title IX clause of the Federal Education Amendments of 1972, which required schools and colleges to spend as much money funding women's sports as men's.

NOT QUITE LIVE TELEVISION.

Until the 1960s when the first TV satellites were launched, there was no live television from the mainland to Hawai'i, so videotapes of regular network programming were flown to the Islands for airing. The CBS Evening News with Walter Cronkite, which aired live at 6:00 p.m. on the East Coast, was taped in Los Angeles at 3:00 p.m. and the tape then flown to Honolulu. With luck, KGMB-TV could put Uncle Walter on the air at 10:30, right after the local news.

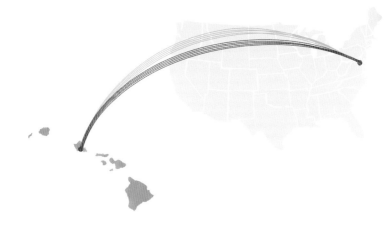

HAWAI'I'S CONGRESSIONAL DELEGATION
ARE FREQUENT FLYERS.

Before serving as governor of Hawai'i for four years, Neil
Abercrombie represented Hawai'i in Congress for ten
two-year terms. During that time, he averaged two trips
every month back home to Honolulu to attend public
meetings, deal with constituent matters and conduct other
official business. After he retired from government, a
rough calculation was made to determine how much time
Abercrombie had spent traveling back and forth between
Honolulu and Washington, DC, during his 20 years in
Congress. Based on flight times of six hours between the
coasts and five hours between the West Coast and Hawai'i,
Abercrombie literally spent one year and three months of
his life in the air!

STATEHOOD FOR HAWAI‘I WAS A TOUGH SELL.

For years before statehood, some in the US Congress believed that Hawai‘i harbored the threat of encroaching Communism, due to the Territory's strong union-dominated workforce. Other members of Congress felt there were just too many non-whites in the voting population. Finally, after a referendum in which 93 percent of Hawai‘i's voters approved statehood, the Territory of Hawai‘i officially became the 50th state on August 21, 1959.

Why 1959 was the most significant year ever for Hawai‘i tourism

- With statehood, mainlanders began to realize that a Hawaiian vacation didn't mean traveling to a strange "foreign" place.

- James Michener's novel *Hawaii* was a blockbuster bestseller, portraying the 50th state as a beautiful, exotic place with a rich history.

- The Boeing 707 was introduced into service. Suddenly travel to Hawai‘i from the West Coast meant a five-hour flight at 30,000 feet—instead of the previous eleven hours in a prop plane at an often bumpy 20,000 feet.

HŌKŪLEʻA
RECREATES HISTORY

In 1975, the Polynesian Voyaging Society launched the double-hulled sailing canoe *Hōkūleʻa*, a full-sized replica of the traditional ocean-going vessels that brought the first Polynesians to Hawaiʻi. The goal was to sail to Tahiti, a 2,700-mile journey almost due south. In 1978, after several sea trials, the first start in rough weather resulting in a swamped canoe in the channel between Oʻahu and Molokaʻi. Crewman and famous big-wave surfer Eddie Aikau was lost attempting to paddle his surfboard to find help. The inaugural Tahitian voyage of *Hōkūleʻa* finally took place in 1978. Using only traditional methods of navigation with no modern instruments, the journey from Hawaiʻi to Tahiti took 35 days. *Hōkūleʻa* has since made many other voyages, including a four-year circumnavigation completed in 2017— calling at 150 ports in 23 countries and territories around the world.

FAST FACT

In 1992 *Hōkūleʻa*, led by Hawaiʻi navigator Nainoa Thompson, radioed in mid-voyage with the orbiting Space Shuttle *Columbia*, manned by Hawaiʻi astronaut Lacy Veach.

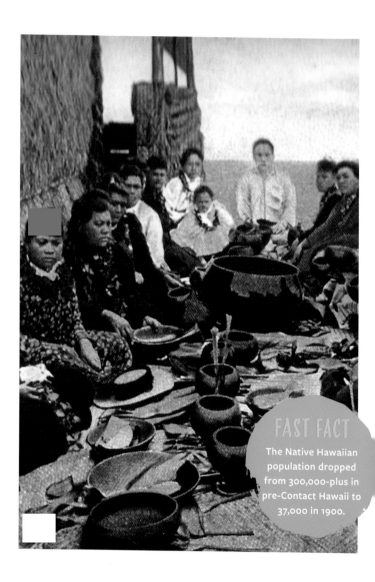

chapter 3

PEOPLE

"We're number 40!"

Despite being the fourth smallest US state in land area (behind Rhode Island, Delaware and Connecticut), Hawai'i has a larger population than ten other states: New Hampshire, Maine, Montana, Rhode Island, Delaware, South Dakota, North Dakota, Alaska, Vermont and Wyoming.

FAST FACT
Nearly two thirds of Hawai'i's 1.5 million people live on O'ahu.

IN HAWAI'I, ONLY NATIVE HAWAIIANS ARE "HAWAIIAN."

Anyone who lives in the Bronx can call himself a New Yorker. But out of respect, islanders without Hawaiian blood don't call themselves Hawaiians. People who were born in Hawai'i, or have lived in the Islands for a very long time, refer to themselves as *kama'aina* (kah-mah-EYE-nah, "child of the land") or more commonly as "local." But only Native Hawaiians, those with Hawaiian blood, are called "Hawaiian."

FOR CENTURIES, HAWAIIANS HAD NO WRITTEN LANGUAGE.

For more than a thousand years after the first South Pacific settlers arrived, the Hawaiian language was spoken only, creating a rich oral tradition in the Islands. When Protestant missionaries began arriving in the early 1800s, they introduced a Hawaiian alphabet, and by the late 1800s Hawaiians were one of the world's most literate peoples. After Hawai'i was annexed by the United States in 1899, teaching the Hawaiian language was forbidden in schools. But in 1978, almost 20 years after Hawai'i became a state, Hawaiian was made the state's second official language, and today a number of immersion schools teach most subjects in the mother tongue.

HOW DO YOU PRONOUNCE IT?

Even if you know only a few Hawaiian words, it's thoughtful and respectful to pronounce them correctly. That's not as hard as it might first appear, thanks to a few basic rules:

FAST FACT

There are only seven consonants in the Hawaiian alphabet: H, K, L, M, N, P and W.

- Vowels are pronounced *ah* (A), *eh* (E), *ee* (I), *oh* (O) and *oo* (U).

- W is sometimes pronounced like a V.

- The *'okina*, which looks like a backward apostrophe, designates a glottal stop—an almost imperceptibly brief break in the pronunciation of a syllable, as in *uh-oh*.

- Every vowel is pronounced.

- The accent falls on the next-to-last syllable of every word.

So now you can pronounce the name of Ka'a'awa, the little community on O'ahu's windward coast. It's kah-ah-AH-vah.

IT'S HAWAI'I'S THIRD "OFFICIAL" LANGUAGE.

Many people in the Islands speak pidgin English, a blend of English and words and phrases from other tongues. Some locals use pidgin a lot, others not so much or not at all. Many can turn it on and off at will, depending on the circumstances or with whom they're conversing. Pidgin is wonderfully colorful and often very funny. For instance, "really delicious" becomes "broke da mout'!" But nothing annoys locals more than hearing someone just off the boat trying to speak pidgin. There's a distinctive lilt to it—an inflection that's not easily replicated.

SHOES OFF WHEN ENTERING ISLAND HOMES.

It's another Asian custom that most everyone observes: Shoes come off before entering someone's home. Sometimes arriving guests will be greeted at the door and told to keep their shoes on, but otherwise removing them on the welcome mat is the best policy. Just remember which pair is yours when you leave—mistaken identity can be a problem, especially with Hawai'i's ubiquitous rubber slippers.

HAWAI'I RESIDENTS ENJOY THE LONGEST LIFE EXPECTANCY IN THE NATION.

The average life expectancy in Hawai'i is 81.3 years, number one in the US. For starters, mostly good weather year-round means more people are outdoors getting some form of exercise. But there's another big reason for this longevity. In the Islands, if you have at least a 20-hour-a-week job, your employer is required to provide health insurance. That's been the State law since 1974 and it clearly pays off.

IN HAWAI'I, EVERYONE'S A MINORITY.

Caucasian 29%   **Hawaiian** 8%

Japanese 18%   **Pacific Islander** 3%

Filipino 14%   **Hispanic** 7%

Chinese 5%   **African American** 3%

Korean 2%   **Other** 4%

Other Asian 7%

Things have changed since the 2010 US census above. According to the Office of Hawaiian Affairs, for instance, there are now more part-Hawaiians, and Filipino residents now surpass Japanese.

BREAKING THE COLOR AND GENDER BARRIERS.

With so many ethnic minorities coexisting in such close quarters, It's no surprise that even Hawai'i has experienced discrimination. Honolulu's exclusive Pacific Club, for example, once had a long tradition of excluding applicants of Asian ancestry. This was a sticky wicket back in the 1970s, when Hawai'i's entire Congressional delegation— two US senators and two House members—were Chinese American or Japanese American. The Pacific Club's restrictions were gender-based, too. Traditionally, women were not accepted as members in their own right. One female executive for a major Honolulu company had her membership application declined after 15 male colleagues from the same company had been accepted. The issue was resolved when the firm's CEO warned that unless she was accepted as a full-fledged member, all of his male executives would resign from the Pacific Club. In 1983 the membership committee finally voted to approve her application with one caveat—she would not be permitted to enter the Card Room.

The importance of being local

In a place whose population has swelled with an influx of people from all over the globe, it has become a mark of distinction to be "local," which can mean either native-born or, depending upon the circumstances, non-white. And even Caucasians, called *haole* (HOW-lee), will make the distinction between a "local haole" born and raised in the Islands and a new arrival who may have had little or no time to assimilate.

PUBLIC SCHOOLS ARE FUNDED BY THE STATE.

Most public schools in the country are funded with
property taxes collected by their cities and towns. Because
there are no municipal governments in Hawai'i, public
education has become the responsibility of the State. Island
public schools generally do a creditable job in the face of
some very unique problems. For instance, English may not
be the primary language for a full quarter of the children
in a sixth grade class. Instead, the language spoken at
home could be the Filipino dialects Tagalog or Ilocano, or
Samoan, or maybe even Chamorro if a family emigrated
from Guam.

HAWAI'I'S PRIVATE SCHOOLS HAVE FLOURISHED.

For a variety of reasons, the Islands boast some of the
best private schools in the country. Hawai'i's top private
secondary schools include Punahou (largest private school
west of the Mississippi and alma mater of Barack Obama),
'Iolani School (excellent college admissions placements
and alma mater of Sun Yat-sen), Kamehameha Schools
(with campuses on four islands and preference given to
children of Hawaiian ancestry), Seabury Hall on Maui,
and Hawai'i Preparatory Academy on the Big Island. All of
these fine schools are K-12, and Kamehameha Schools also
has 29 preschools statewide.

Celebrities Love Hawaii

CHARLES LINDBERGH, the famed aviator, chose Maui as his final resting place. He is buried on the eastern end of the island near the town of Hāna, on the grounds of Palapala Hoʻomau Church.

ARTHUR GODFREY, a popular radio and television personality in the 1940s and '50s, helped launch the boom in Hawaiʻi tourism. Godfrey frequently played the *ʻukulele* on his radio and TV broadcasts and often featured a hula dancer on his weekly television program.

ELVIS PRESLEY made three motion pictures on location in the Islands (*Blue Hawaii*; *Paradise, Hawaiian Style*; *Girls! Girls! Girls!*), starred in a 1973 Honolulu TV special that was the first program ever beamed around the world by satellite

(Elvis: Aloha From Hawaii) and staged a benefit concert that raised funds to help build the Arizona Memorial at Pearl Harbor.

JIM NABORS, the veteran singer and television actor, best known for his Gomer Pyle character on *The Andy Griffith Show*, performed in Waikīkī in the 1980s and was a full-time Hawai'i resident until his death in 2017 at age 87.

DORIS DUKE, the tobacco heiress, built Shangri-La, her elaborate home with a private harbor, on the water at the foot of Diamond Head. The house is now a museum featuring Islamic art, culture and design.

JACK LORD, the actor best remembered for his role as Steve McGarrett in the original *Hawaii Five-O* television series, was a full-time permanent Honolulu resident who died in 1998, leaving his entire estate, estimated at $40 million, to local charities.

THE KINGSTON TRIO helped start the 1950s folk music phenomenon—in 1959 the group had four albums in the top ten at the same time! Two of its original members, **Bob Shane** and **Dave Guard**, were born and raised in the Islands, where they attended Punahou School.

BETTE MIDLER was a military dependent who attended O'ahu's Radford High School and the University of Hawai'i, where she starred in a production of *South Pacific* before launching her professional career. She also played a seasick missionary in the motion picture *Hawai'i*.

ELLISON ONIZUKA, a Big Island native son and to date the only American astronaut of Asian ancestry, was killed in the tragic explosion of the space shuttle *Challenger* in 1986. The Big Island's international airport on the Kona Coast is now named for him.

BARACK OBAMA was born in Honolulu, graduated from Punahou School and served as a senator from Illinois and the 44th president of the United States.

JAMES MICHENER wrote the bestselling novel *Hawaii* that was published in 1959 and became the hit movie of the same name.

STEVE CASE, born and raised in Hawai'i, co-founded AOL and rose to prominence in the tech industry, becoming chairman and CEO of AOL/Time Warner Communications.

CLARE BOOTHE LUCE was an actress, author, playwright, politician, US ambassador and the wife of Time-Life publisher Henry Luce. For many years she kept a lavish home on Honolulu's Kāhala Beach, where she hosted celebrities, captains of industry and US presidents.

HENRY J. KAISER, the innovative industrialist whose WWII shipyards turned out Liberty Ships at the rate of one a day to carry supplies and equipment to Europe, owned TV and radio stations in Honolulu, built what is now the Hilton Hawaiian Village Waikīkī Beach Resort (originally the Kaiser Hawaiian Village Hotel) and developed one of Hawai'i's largest residential-commercial communities— Hawai'i Kai in East Honolulu.

JAMES MACARTHUR, the son of actress Helen Hayes, starred with Jack Lord in the original version of *Hawaii Five-O*. Book 'em, Danno!

CHARLIE CHAN, the fictional Chinese-American detective created by author Earl Derr Biggers, was fictional, of course, but was based on Chang Apana, a real-life Honolulu police detective in the early 20th century.

Many other celebrities, from **Roseanne Barr** to **Dwayne "The Rock" Johnson** to **Mark Zuckerberg**, have family ties to Hawai'i or own property in the Islands, with Maui being a particular favorite. Among that island's part-time residents: **Willie Nelson**, **Oprah Winfrey**, **Owen Wilson**, **Woody Harrelson**, **Kris Kristofferson**, and rockers **Pat Simmons** of the Doobie Brothers, **Mick Fleetwood** of Fleetwood Mac and **Steven Tyler** of Aerosmith.

FAST FACT

Hawai'i plays host to some ten million visitors a year—about 250,000 of them in the Islands on any given day.

FAST FACT

In 2009 'ukulele virtuoso Jake Shimabukuro and Hawai'i's Bette Midler performed a duet before Queen Elizabeth II.

chapter

4

MUSIC

The 'ukulele isn't originally from Hawai'i.

When the Mexican *vaqueros* came to Hawai'i to teach the locals how to handle cattle, they brought their guitars along. And when the Portuguese arrived to work on the sugar and pineapple plantations, they brought a stringed instrument called a *braguinha*, which eventually evolved into the 'ukulele.

HAWAI'I'S FIRST HEAVY METAL.

The weepy, emblematic steel guitar sound that punctuates so many Hawaiian songs was introduced around 1900 by young Joseph Kekuku, while walking one day in Honolulu with his guitar. Picking up a rusty iron bolt lying on the ground, Kekuku accidentally dropped it onto his guitar strings. He liked the sound so much that he experimented by sliding a pocket knife and then a steel comb along the strings, and finally a polished steel bar like the ones steel guitarists use today. Over the years, the instrument was adopted and popularized by musicians from coast to coast, most notably the legendary guitar virtuoso Jerry Byrd.

IT'S THE KEY TO CONTEMPORARY ISLAND MUSIC.

Slack key (*kī hō'alu*), a Hawaiian guitar style using open tunings, dates back to the 19th century, when those vaqueros imported the instrument and Hawaiians created new tunings to suit their own musical styles and harmonies. In slack key, guitar strings are loosened slightly (slackened), then retuned to produce basic chords, freeing the musician to press individual strings for the melody—in effect, allowing him to accompany himself. Individual tunings could be closely guarded in Hawaiian families, and the first slack key recordings weren't made until 1946, when the legendary Island musician Gabby Pahinui cut a series of records. The genre enjoyed a surge of popularity in the 1960s and '70s and is now a key ingredient in contemporary Hawaiian music.

NOT EVERYONE LOVES HAPA HAOLE MUSIC.

In Hawaiian, *hapa* means "part" and haole originally meant "foreigner." Dating back more than a century, hapa haole music is a kind of Tin Pan Alley take on Island songs, with styling or subject matter that's Hawaiian, but lyrics mostly or entirely in English. It's really a separate genre of Hawai'i music, and in some quarters considered a misappropriation of Hawaiian culture. Examples range from classics like "Sweet Leilani" and "Lovely Hula Hands" to laughers like "Yaaka Hula Hickey Dula" and "They're

Wearing 'Em Higher in Hawaya" (a reference to grass skirts), both published back in 1916.

THE WORLD'S HIGHEST PAID DISC JOCKEY.

From the early '50s to the early '80s, Brooklyn native J. Akuhead Pupule—born Herschel Hohenstein, a name he later had legally changed to Hal Lewis—earned big bucks as a morning disk jockey at several Honolulu radio stations, where he invariably sat high atop the ratings year after year. Earning $100,000 in 1955 and a much higher salary later in his career, "Aku" was purported to be the highest paid disk jockey in the world, a claim that was never seriously disputed.

DON HO BEFORE "TINY BUBBLES."

Before he became the sleepy-eyed, laid-back entertainer who made "Tiny Bubbles" a classic, Don Ho was a standout football player for the University of Hawai'i and an Air Force jet pilot who crash-landed on a training mission in Texas and walked away without a scratch.

WHO'S THAT

singing

"OVER THE RAINBOW/
WHAT A WONDERFUL WORLD?"

You hear it everywhere, from movie soundtracks to
elevator music. First popularized in the 1986 film
Meet Joe Black and Toys 'R Us commercials, Israel
Kamakawiwoʻole's distinctive mega-hit has won a
boatload of national awards and sold some five million
digital downloads. The medley was recorded in a
single take at three in the morning, on a spur-of-the-
moment whim by the beloved, and exceptionally obese,
Hawaiian singer. (At one point, "Bruddah Iz" tipped the
scales at more than 750 pounds.) When Iz died in 1997
at age 38, he lay in state in Honolulu's State Capitol
Building, only the third person so honored—and the
only one who wasn't a government official.

THE FIRE KNIFE DANCE IS NOT AN ANCIENT POLYNESIAN ART FORM.

This spirited staple of the South Seas revue was actually created in 1948 by Samoan chief Olo Letuli, a sometime Hawai'i resident who had taken his traditional knife dance to a Shriners convention in San Francisco. Watching other performers practice their routines in Golden Gate Park, Chief Letuli spotted a baton twirler with light bulbs on either end of her baton and nearby, a Hindu fire eater. Inspired, he tied fabric strips to the end of his Samoan knives, doused them in kerosene borrowed from the fire eater, and the rest is musical history. Today the Samoan fire knife dance is an art form practiced around the globe, and the annual World Fireknife Championships, held since 1993 at O'ahu's Polynesian Cultural Center, include a division for dancers as young as six years old.

HAWAIIAN MUSIC AROUND THE WORLD.

How far has Hawaiian music traveled? A group called the Boxcar Hawaiian Toasties tours the Czech Republic and elsewhere in Eastern Europe, playing their version of Hawaiian music with a guitar, a double bass, an ukulele and a steel guitar. That's how far!

FAST FACT

By law, no building on Kaua'i can be higher than the tallest palm tree.

chapter
5

BUSINESS

The Big Five meant business.

For generations, they controlled commerce, government and even much of the culture of the Hawaiian Islands. Founded by the descendants of American missionaries and traders, the "Big Five" was an all-powerful fraternity of companies: Alexander & Baldwin, Castle & Cooke, C. Brewer & Company, Amfac and Theo H. Davies. They started in sugar and pineapple, expanded into shipping, and together become the major force in Hawai'i's economy—and on the political scene under the auspices of the Republican Party. The power and influence of the Big Five began to wane in the postwar years and with the advent of statehood, when the Democratic party wrested control of Island government from the Republicans—and, for the most part, have held it ever since. Today only Alexander & Baldwin and Castle & Cooke still operate as those corporate entities in the Islands.

AGRICULTURE NO LONGER FUELS HAWAI'I'S ECONOMY.

For more than 150 years, the Island economy revolved around agriculture. Sprawling sugar plantations flourished on O'ahu, Maui, Kaua'i and the Big Island, and much of Moloka'i and Lāna'i were given over to pineapple. But nearly all of them closed in the face of competition from the Philippines and Latin America, where companies like Del Monte and Dole could pay field workers a fraction of the hourly rates commanded by Hawai'i's unionized workforce.

FAST FACT

Once the world's largest pineapple plantation, Lāna'i is now 97% owned by Oracle Corporation founder Larry Ellison.

THE LAST SUGAR HARVEST.

Maui was the home of Hawaiʻi's last sugar plantation, operated by Alexander & Baldwin subsidiary Hawaiian Commercial & Sugar Company. Whenever you emptied a little packet of Sugar in the Raw into your coffee, it was Maui sugar. HC&S closed for good in December of 2016, when the plantation's big yellow cane haul trucks brought the last loads of cut sugarcane to the Puʻunēnē Mill in central Maui, after 147 years of continuous operation.

CATTLE RANCHING IS A 150-YEAR-OLD TRADITION IN THE ISLANDS.

In 1793, the British explorer and navigator George Vancouver arrived in Hawaiʻi with a gift for King Kamehameha I—a small herd of cattle, six cows and a bull. The king carved out a pasture enclosed by a rock wall and placed a *kapu* on the cattle to ensure they wouldn't be killed. As a result, over the next half century more than 25,000 long-horned cattle were roaming wild and had become a very real nuisance. King Kamehameha III lifted the *kapu*, new ranches were established, and Spanish *vaquero* were brought in to teach the Hawaiians how to manage cattle. In fact, there were cowboys in the Islands even before the great cattle drives of the American West. Cowboys in Hawaiʻi are called *paniolo* (pah-nee-OH-lo), derived from the Spanish *español*.

BUT GRAZING LANDS ARE
shrinking

These days, depending on the economy and the weather, there are between 800 and 1,000 ranches on five of Hawai'i's eight main islands. (There's no minimum number of cattle that constitutes a ranch. Got a couple of cows and a horse? You've got a ranch.) As the state's population has grown, ranch lands have diminished. In 1937, two million acres were designated as "grazing land" in the Islands. In 2015, only 750,000 acres were classified as "pasture."

"WHO ARE THESE GUYS?"

In 1908 three paniolo from the Big Island's Pu'uwa'awa'a Ranch entered the Frontier Days championship rodeo in Cheyenne, Wyoming, then the premier rodeo in the country. Some 12,000 spectators watched Hawaiian cowboy Ikua Purdy beat the best in the West to win the steer roping event. Two other Hawaiians, their cowboy hats adorned with flower *lei*, won third and sixth place in the event. According to the Cheyenne newspaper, the three men from Hawai'i "took the breath of the American cowboys."

SOME LIVESTOCK TRAVEL TO AND FROM HAWAI'I—BY PLANE.

Most of the calves raised by Hawai'i ranches are sent to feedlots on the mainland for fattening. Most go by ship, but about 5,000 go by air each year. Twice a month, a jumbo Boeing 747 flies livestock—mostly cattle and some horses—in both directions between Los Angeles and either Honolulu or Kailua-Kona on the Big Island. Lightweight portable stalls are secured in the aircraft to accommodate the four-legged passengers, and a veterinarian technician is always on board. Capacity is approximately 200 head, and the one-way cost is about 50 cents a pound for cattle and $3,300 for horses.

WHY AREN'T THERE INTER-ISLAND PASSENGER FERRIES IN HAWAI'I?

Back in the 1970s, the hydrofoil operator SeaFlite carried passengers between O'ahu and Maui. SeaFlite's three sleek Jetfoils could attain over-water speeds of about 50 mph, but the notoriously rough Kaiwi Channel between O'ahu and Moloka'i caused mechanical breakdowns and seasick passengers. Beset by financial problems, Seaflite went out of business after only two years, its Jetfoils sold to a Hong Kong company for service in calmer waters. Then in 2007, a larger, more user-friendly vessel called the Hawai'i Superferry began running between Honolulu Harbor and Maui and Kaua'i. The Superferry could carry cars, trucks and people, but met with considerable opposition from environmental organizations and outrigger canoe clubs, among others. The comfortable craft performed well, but the company stopped operations after the Hawai'i Supreme Court ruled it hadn't met all the requirements for completing an environmental impact statement. The Superferry finally filed for Chapter 11 bankruptcy in 2009.

FAST FACT

On March 6, 1979, a Hawaiian Airlines flight from Honolulu to Moloka'i made history as the first certified scheduled American airliner "manned" by an all-female crew—pilot, co-pilot and flight attendant.

SHIPPING COSTS AFFECT JUST ABOUT EVERYTHING.

Transportation is the one factor that impacts nearly everyone's cost of living. You name it and chances are it comes by boat— from cars to corn flakes and everything in between. Major shipper Matson Navigation Co., for instance, brings upwards of 150,000 container loads and 65,000 new cars to the Islands every year. Furthermore, most of those huge cargo vessels return empty—since Hawai'i's last sugar plantation closed in 2016 and pineapple is now mostly grown for local consumption. On the Neighbor Islands (Kaua'i, Maui, Moloka'i, Lāna'i and the Big Island), almost all incoming goods must be transshipped in Honolulu. Such cargo usually gets to its Neighbor Island destinations on barges— huge floating warehouses.

CALL IT THE PRICE OF PARADISE.

Hawai'i's cost of living is not for the faint of heart. In addition to lofty transportation costs, there's the high cost of land and housing. These days, the median price for single family homes on O'ahu runs upwards of $800,000, while a small retail property on Waikīkī's pricey Kalākaua Avenue recently sold for more than $16,000 per square foot for the land and more than $10,000 per square foot for the building.

GAS PRICES ARE HIGHER TOO.

There are two oil refineries on Oʻahu, but the crude oil must still be imported from afar, usually from Asia. Typically, the price of gas at the pump is about a dollar more per gallon than it is on the US mainland. To meet demand, about 40 million gallons of crude oil are transported to Hawaiʻi each year—brought in by as many as 95 oil tankers.

ONCE THERE WERE TRAINS.

In addition to transporting workers into the fields, little narrow-gauge trains hauled fresh-cut sugar cane to the mills and fresh-picked pineapples to the canneries. On the Big Island's Hāmākua Coast, the Hawaiʻi Consolidated Railway connected plantation communities for 34 cliff-hugging miles, from Hilo to the little town of Paʻauilo. Today a beautifully restored locomotive from Maui's Lahaina Kaanapali & Pacific Railroad (LKPRR) is on display at the Smithsonian Institution in Washington, DC. The LKPRR still runs its Sugar Cane Train tours on a limited seasonal basis.

AMERICA'S ONLY

coffee

GROWING STATE

Coffee being a tropical crop, Hawai'i is the only state in the Union where commercially viable coffee is grown. Hawaiian coffee, in fact, is recognized around the world as one of the best premium brews on the market today. While Kona coffee gets most of the press, excellent specialty coffees are grown and produced on 9,000 acres on O'ahu, Maui, Kaua'i, Moloka'i and the Big Island. Making the most of the volcanic soil, balmy temperatures, and just the right combination of morning sun and afternoon showers, nearly 1,000 farms contribute to making coffee the state's second highest value crop—right behind seed corn.

HAWAI'I LEADS THE WORLD IN SPAM® CONSUMPTION.

Approximately seven million cans of SPAM® are sold in Hawai'i each year (a throwback to WWII when fresh meat was in short supply and many local households had no refrigerators). That's almost five cans for every man, woman and child in the state. Much of it goes into the signature snack called Spam musubi (MOO-soo-bee), basically a slice of the luncheon meat placed on a rectangle of sticky rice and wrapped in nori, a dried seaweed.

IT'S THE "OFFICIAL" STATE PASTRY.

Originally brought to Hawai'i by Portuguese immigrants, the malasada is a tennis ball-sized lump of dough that's deep-fat fried and rolled in sugar. Malasadas are best eaten in the car on the way home from the bakery, while they're still warm. Just how popular are hot malasadas? Leonard's Bakery, doing business in Honolulu since 1952, estimates they sell about 10,000 malasadas every Sunday morning!

Hawai'i is a major player on the silver screen.

Over the past century the Islands have starred in or had stand-in roles in more than 100 motion pictures, beginning with silent films like *The White Flower* (1923) and *Hula* (1927), in which "It Girl" Clara Bow, playing a character named Hula Calhoun, had a nude swimming scene and Olympic champion Duke Kahanamoku made a cameo appearance. Among other notable movies shot in Hawai'i:

Waikiki Wedding (1937)

From Here to Eternity (1953)

South Pacific (1958)

The Old Man and the Sea (1958)

Gidget Goes Hawaiian (1961)

Blue Hawaii (1961)

In Harm's Way (1965)

Hawaii (1966)

Raiders of the Lost Ark (1981)

Throw Momma from the Train (1987)

Jurassic Park (1993)

Waterworld (1995)

Outbreak (1995)

Pearl Harbor (2001)

Planet of the Apes (2001)

Tears of the Sun (2003)

50 First Dates (2004)

Tropic Thunder (2008)

Forgetting Sarah Marshall (2008)

Avatar (2009)

Pirates of the Caribbean: On Stranger Tides (2011)

The Descendants (2011)

The Hunger Games: Catching Fire (2013)

Godzilla (2014)

Jurassic World (2015)

Jumanji: Welcome to the Jungle (2017)

Kong: Skull Island (2017)

And Hawai'i on the small screen.

There's more to Hawai'i TV shows than Steve McGarrett and Thomas Magnum. First out of the box was the detective series *Hawaiian Eye*, which debuted in 1958 in black and white and ran for four seasons. Since then Hawai'i has played many a featured role or—with its diverse climatic zones and attractive tax incentives for filmmakers—has stood in for locales in Africa, Asia, Europe, South America and other locations worldwide. Two of Hawai'i's longest-running TV shows—*Hawaii Five-O* and *Magnum, P.I.*—have even been revived in encore series. On the tube from the tropics:

Aloha Paradise	*Dog the Bounty Hunter*
Baywatch Hawaii	*Fantasy Island*
Beyond the Break	*Follow the Sun*
Big Wave Dave's	*Gilligan's Island*
Byrds of Paradise	*Hawaii Five-O*
Charlie's Angels	*Hawaii*
China Beach	*Hawaiian Eye*

Hawaiian Heat	*Raven*
Island Son	*The Brian Keith Show*
Jake and the Fatman	*The Diamond Head Game*
Lost	*The Don Ho Show*
Magnum, P.I.	*The MacKenzies of Paradise Cove*
North Shore	
One West Waikiki	*The River*
Paradise Run	*The Thorn Birds*

THERE ARE NO

BILLBOARDS

IN HAWAI'I.

In fact, there's almost no outdoor advertising. A company is only permitted to advertise at its actual place of business and even then the law specifies how big the sign can be in proportion to the size of the building. What's more, no signs visible from the street are permitted above the second floor. The credit goes to The Outdoor Circle, a community organization founded in 1912 to help preserve Hawai'i's natural beauty.

FAST FACT

The Hawaiian monk seal (with the hoary bat) is one of only two mammals endemic to Hawai'i.

chapter
6

NATURE

Hawai'i has every type of climate found on Earth.

With terrain extending from sea level to more than 14,000 feet in elevation, the Islands boast all five of the world's climate categories: tropical, dry, temperate, cold and polar. Lying some 20 degrees north of the equator, Hawai'i has a climate that's classified as tropical at or near sea level and subtropical at higher elevations.

THE WEATHER CHANGES CONSTANTLY.

Summer days are mostly sunny with occasional brief afternoon showers. The winter months, roughly December through March, bring considerably more rain. And because the islands are mountainous, there are often micro-climates around each of the major islands. On Maui, for instance, it can be raining hard in Makawao, but bright and sunny in the Lahaina area. The one constant are the trade winds—sometimes light, sometimes blustery—that blow out of the northeast some 350 days a year.

HOW CLIMATE CHANGE AFFECTS HAWAIʻI.

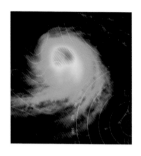

A half century ago, hurricanes nearly always passed well south of the Hawaiian Islands. But as the Pacific Ocean began to warm, these storms became more powerful and started coming closer. In September 1992, Hurricane Iniki was heading due west and passing safely below the island chain when it suddenly turned almost due north and made a direct hit on Kauaʻi. The eye of the storm, with sustained winds of more than 145 mph, hovered over the island for three quarters of an hour, during which time Iniki generated the equivalent of 30 years of trash. Nearly 1,500 homes were destroyed and more than 5,000 suffered major damage. Producer Steven Spielberg, on Kauaʻi wrapping up location shooting for *Jurassic Park*, included his movie crew's storm footage in the finished film.

NOT ALL OF HAWAIʻI'S WAVES ARE FOR SURFING.

Most tsunamis generated in the Islands or by earthquakes around the Pacific Rim wreak little or no damage. But on April 1, 1946, a tsunami powered by a temblor in the Aleutian Islands hit Hawaiʻi with little warning and terrible results, especially in the Big Island town of Hilo, where 173 people were killed and 163 injured, with almost 500 buildings destroyed and nearly 1,000 others damaged. The warnings came too late, and even then many residents believed them to be an April Fool's Day prank. This disaster prompted creation of the Pacific Tsunami Warning Center at Pearl Harbor, which now issues warnings and updates to Hawai'i and countries around the Pacific.

O'ahu's upside-down waterfalls

Drive along the Pali Highway through Honolulu's Nu'uanu Valley after a heavy rain, and you can sometimes see waterfalls spilling over the cliffs, then being blown right back up into the air by strong updrafts on the high valley walls.

DON'T CALL IT SMOG.

That haze in the air on some days is probably vog, a hybrid name given to volcanic smog drifting over from Kīlauea, the Big Island volcano that's been erupting almost nonstop since 1983. People on the Island of Hawai'i see more vog, of course, but, depending on the wind, there are days when a light haze can also reach Maui, Moloka'i and O'ahu.

HAWAI'I IS THE WORLD'S ENDANGERED SPECIES CAPITAL.

Sad but true: Nowhere else on the planet are more plants, birds and animals in danger of extinction—more than 25 percent of the endangered species in the US. This is due in large part to the high number of endemic species found nowhere else in the world. On this list of dubious distinction are hundreds of species of reptiles, waterfowl, insects, snails and mammals: the Hawaiian hoary bat, Laysan duck, 'alalā (Hawaiian crow), O'ahu tree snail, Kaua'i cave wolf spider, Hawaiian monk seal and *honu*, or green sea turtle. (A half-century ago, the honu was still found on menus in Island restaurants.) Many Hawaiian bird species have already gone the way of the dodo, including the Lāna'i hookbill, the greater *koa* finch and the Moloka'i creeper.

HOW NOT TO COOK YOUR GOOSE.

Even Hawai'i's state bird, the *nēnē* goose, had dwindled to a few dozen survivors by the late 1950s. But several breeding pairs were captured and nurtured, and as their numbers slowly increased, the nēnē were gradually reintroduced into the wild, primarily on Maui and Hawai'i Island. Today, the official estimate puts the number of nēnē at more than a thousand on the Big Island and twice that number on the upper slopes of Maui's Haleakalā volcano.

THERE ARE NO VENOMOUS LAND SNAKES IN HAWAI'I.

It's one reason there are so many birds in the Islands: no snakes slithering up into the trees to eat their eggs. But there's always concern about the brown tree snake, which is a big problem on Guam, the Micronesian island 4,000 miles to the west. There, the bird population has been decimated by brown tree snakes, which also crawl up utility poles and cause frequent electrical brown-outs. In Hawai'i, State inspectors meet every flight and every container ship arriving from Guam to check for slithery stowaways. Hawai'i does have one tiny import called the brahminy blind snake, which is non-venomous and looks more like an earthworm. And fortunately for swimmers and divers, sightings of Hawai'i's poisonous yellow-bellied sea snake are few and far between.

SO WHAT CRITTERS *DO* CALL HAWAI'I HOME?

Even without venomous snakes, there's still plenty of wildlife out in the bush. Land mammals include Axis deer, mule deer, black tail deer, mountain goats, Mouflon sheep, wild boars, Indian mongooses, rats and mice, wild donkeys on the Big Island, wild rabbits on tiny off-lying islands and even a small colony of wallabies in O'ahu's Kalihi Valley.

THE SONG OF THE NIGHTINGALE.

Those Big Island donkeys are called "Kona nightingales"—descendants of the livestock that once worked Hawai'i's coffee farms. Still wandering the lava fields of West Hawai'i, the now-feral Kona nightingales are so named for their distinctive nocturnal braying.

THOSE WILD BOARS CAN MAKE PIGS OF THEMSELVES.

Wild boars, found on all of Hawai'i's main islands, cause serious damage to vegetation by digging up soil in search of earthworms and roots to eat. Weighing up to 650 pounds, they can also be aggressive and extremely dangerous if they feel threatened. Permitted hunting helps control Hawai'i's feral pig population.

MONGOOSES BY DAY, RATS BY NIGHT.

In 1883, as rats became a nagging problem for Hawai'i's nascent sugar industry, plantation managers imported mongooses from India to eradicate them. Unfortunately, they overlooked one small detail: Rats are nocturnal, but mongooses are diurnal. So while the rat continued to proliferate, so did the mongoose. As local tour bus drivers like to tell their passengers, the rat and the mongoose are now just neighbors who pass each other on the way to work.

THERE ARE NO PRIVATE BEACHES IN HAWAI'I.

All beaches in the Islands are owned by the state—every beach on every island, extending all the way up to the high-water mark. That includes the beaches in front of the swankiest hotels.

Why are there thousands of wild chickens running all over Kaua'i?

When Hurricane 'Iwa struck the island of Kaua'i in 1982, thousands of homes were badly damaged or destroyed, and flimsy chicken coops were no match for the storm's 140-mph winds. Most were literally blown away, chickens and all. Today, the descendants of those birds can be seen roaming free island-wide.

HAWAI'I IS THE ONLY STATE THAT'S RABIES-FREE.

If you're thinking of bringing your dog or cat to the Islands, be aware of the mandatory minimum five-day quarantine— and that's only if your pet meets all the requirements for checkups and shots before leaving home. Otherwise the quarantine period is 120 days. There are certain exemptions for service dogs or pets arriving from rabies-free countries.

Long-Distance

HUMPBACK WHALES

Each year, North Pacific humpback whales migrate from Alaskan waters to Hawai'i, spending the winter months in and around its 1,400-square-mile national marine sanctuary. The whales eat nothing while in Hawaiian waters, where the females give birth to their calves, losing a third of their body weight in the process. Estimates are that some 12,000 whales visit the Islands roughly between November and April.

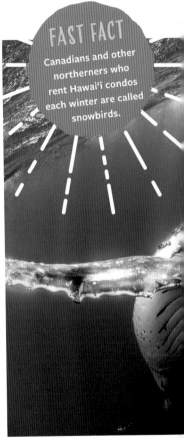

FAST FACT

Canadians and other northerners who rent Hawai'i condos each winter are called snowbirds.

Migrations

The **kolea**, or Pacific golden plover, migrates every year between Hawai'i and Alaska, a 3,000-mile nonstop flight over open ocean, always leaving right on schedule in late April. Remarkably, when each kolea makes the three-day return flight to Hawai'i in the fall, it comes back to the same spot—the same backyard or pasture or golf course fairway that it left in the spring.

FAST FACT

The Eddie Aikau Big Wave Invitational is held at Waimea Bay only when wave faces are consistently 30 feet or more.

chapter

7

SPORTS

Where are Hawai'i's biggest waves?

When the surf's up in Hawai'i, it's really *up*! Winter brings the biggest waves to most of the state's north and west shores, but for surfing's elite the destination of choice is Pe'ahi on Maui, also known as Jaws, where 50- and 60-foot waves are the ultimate challenge. With such monster waves, too big and fast to catch by traditional hand paddling, doughty surfers are towed into the waves by a line attached to a Jet Ski or even a helicopter. On O'ahu's fabled North Shore, another tow-in surf mecca is Log Cabins on the outer reef, where rideable waves have been reported as high as 80 feet.

HAWAI'S SURFERS MEASURE WAVES DIFFERENTLY.

Why is a six-foot wave at Chun's Reef on the North Shore bigger than an eight-foot wave at Maverick's in California? Because Island surfers measure the size of a wave from the highest point, called the peak, to an imaginary spot in the water if the ocean were flat. Everyone else in the world measures from the peak to the trough, the lowest point. Hawai'i surfers believe the latter method would needlessly exaggerate the size of their waves, which are already impressive enough.

HAWAIIAN ROYALTY HELPED EXPORT SURFING.

We'll never know who invented surfing. The art of *he'e nalu*, or "wave sliding" as the ancient Hawaiians called it, was practiced throughout Polynesia long before first European contact. But it was Hawaiians who introduced the sport in California and laid the foundation for today's international surfing culture. Back in 1885, three Island princes away at boarding school, including future Congressional delegate Prince Kūhiō, first rode the waves at Santa Cruz on their custom redwood boards. Thirty years later, Olympic swimming champion Duke Kahanamoku took a break from Australian swimming exhibitions to hit the surf in Sydney before stoked spectators witnessing surfing for the first time.

WHY THEY CALL DUKE KAHANAMOKU HAWAI'I'S GREATEST ATHLETE.

Descended from Hawaiian nobility, Honolulu native Duke Paoa Kahanamoku (1890-1968) was a master of the 100-meter men's freestyle swimming event, in which he won a total of three gold and two silver medals in four Olympic games. While Duke did much to popularize surfing and turn it into a major international sport, he was also a bona fide hero. In 1925 he saved the lives of eight people, bringing them to shore on his surfboard after their fishing boat capsized off Corona Del Mar, California. Duke's heroics that day prompted the use of surfboards as ocean rescue gear for US lifeguards.

DUKE RODE A MILE-LONG WAVE AT WAIKĪKĪ—ON A BOARD WITH NO SKEG.

In 1917, 26-year-old Duke caught a wave he estimated at between 25 and 30 feet high at the Castle's surf break, which lies far out near the deep shipping channel off of Waikīkī Beach—a spot that only breaks on big-surf days. His board was a 16-foot, 114-pound redwood plank without a skeg—surfboard fins hadn't yet been invented. The wave diminished in size as he surfed nonstop toward shore for a mile through several successive surf breaks—Public's, Cunha's, Queens and Canoes—until finally stepping ashore

FAST FACT

October's 41-mile race from Moloka'i to O'ahu, is the world championship of outrigger canoe racing, even drawing clubs from Europe and China.

not far from where his bronze statue (previous page) stands today. This remarkable feat was immortalized seven years later in Robert Ripley's "Believe It Or Not."

FROM IRRIGATION DITCH TO OLYMPIC PODIUM.

In the 1930s Soichi Sakamoto was an unassuming science teacher who taught students to swim in the sugarcane irrigation ditches of Puʻunēnē, Maui. Not a strong swimmer himself, Sakamoto coached his kids to greatness with revolutionary, science-based swimming techniques that have become standard practice today. Many of the plantation kids he coached in the cane ditches went on to become national and international champions, including Keo Nakama, who set a world record in the mile swim, and Bill Smith, who won Olympic gold in the 400-meter and 800-meter freestyle relays at the 1948 Games in London.

AND YOU THOUGHT THE TOUR DE FRANCE WAS TOUGH!

Each year in June Maui hosts a bicycle race unlike any other. The Cycle to the Sun begins at sea level in the little town of Pāʻia; the finish line is at the 10,029-foot summit of Maui's Haleakalā volcano. This grueling, three-hour-plus competition is a 36-mile climb with gradients of up to 18 percent along the way.

THE HONOLULU MARATHON IS THE FOURTH LARGEST IN THE US.

In fact, it's one of the biggest in the world, attracting more than 30,000 participants every December to run, walk or hobble the 26.2-mile course along Honolulu's scenic southern shoreline, from Kaka'ako out to the suburb of Hawai'i Kai and back to Waikīkī's Kapi'olani Park. Dating back to 1973, the Honolulu Marathon is a favorite of elite runners from all over the world. Typically, about half the entrants hail from Japan.

GAME CALLED ON ACCOUNT OF WAR.

In late November 1941, the San Jose State Spartans football team boarded the *SS Lurline* for the five-day cruise from San Francisco to Honolulu, where they were scheduled to play exhibition games at Honolulu Stadium against the University of Hawai'i and Willamette College. But the game was cancelled when the Japanese attacked Pearl Harbor a few days after they arrived. Players were forced to remain in Honolulu for four weeks, when many of them were finally able to sail home aboard the *SS Coolidge*, pressed into service as sailors and ambulance attendants. Four of the players opted to remain in the Islands, where they signed on as members of the Honolulu Police Department.

MICHIGAN STATE'S BAREFOOT KICKER.

Hawai'i children love going barefoot—for years, kids weren't required to wear shoes to school until the seventh grade. But Dick Kenney learned to kick a football barefoot, as both a punter and a placekicker. It was no big deal in Hawai'i when he was a star player at 'Iolani School, but it made sports headlines when he helped Michigan State to national championships in 1965 and '66, kicking barefoot in rain, sleet or snow. The Spartans' 1964 win over the University of Southern California, in which Kenney kicked a 49-yard field goal with no shoes on, was the first mainland athletic event televised live in the Islands.

BABE RUTH AND THE VOLCANO.

In 1933, nearing the end of his career, Babe Ruth played exhibition games on O'ahu, where he lofted a trademark swat over Honolulu Stadium's right field fence, and on the Big Island, where he batted autographed baseballs into the caldera of Kīlauea volcano. A year later, the Bambino was back in the Islands for more exhibition games with New York Yankee teammates Lou Gehrig, Jimmie Foxx and Lefty Gomez.

WHY IS THE (DISPUTED)

Father of Baseball

BURIED IN A HAWAI'I CEMETERY?

Alexander Joy Cartwright, who founded the New York Knickerbocker Base Ball Club in 1842, shares the mantle of inventor of the modern sport with Abner Doubleday, in a historical disagreement that is still hotly disputed by baseball geeks. In 1849 Cartwright headed west to join the California gold rush and then continued on to the Kingdom of Hawai'i, where he introduced baseball, served as an advisor to King Kalākaua and saw duty as Honolulu's fire chief from 1850 to 1863. Cartwright died in Honolulu in 1892 and was buried in O'ahu Cemetery. To this day, a group of several dozen baseball fans gather there every April 17 to serenade him with "Happy Birthday to You" and "Take Me Out to the Ball Game."

JOE DIMAGGIO HIT IT OUT OF THE PARK TOO.

During WWII "Joltin' Joe" was a staff sergeant in the US Air Force, assigned to Hickam Field to help build morale. DiMaggio reportedly felt he was being exploited but still played in several exhibition games, along with other former major league ballplayers who had also joined the armed forces. In June 1944, the Yankee Clipper electrified a crowd of 22,000 with a 435-foot home run over the Honolulu Stadium fence and into the front yard of philanthropist August Dreier's mansion across the street. For many years this towering homer stood as the longest home run hit out of the old ballpark.

FAST FACT

At age 40, Keo Nakama became the first person to swim the 27-mile Kaiwi Channel from Moloka'i to O'ahu, making the crossing in 15-1/2 hours.

TOUGH LOSS FOR AN ISLANDER PITCHER.

No-hitters are rare in baseball at the professional level, but Dave Freisleben had an even rarer experience as a Hawaii Islanders pitcher. On June 2, 1973, he pitched a no-hitter against the Albuquerque Dukes—then lost the game when he walked in the winning run.

Hawai'i was once a member of the world's biggest professional sports league.

In 1961 minor league baseball came to the Islands when the Sacramento Solons moved to Honolulu and became the Hawaii Islanders of the Pacific Coast League. That officially made the PCL the biggest league in professional sports, geographically speaking, stretching 4,350 miles from Honolulu to Indianapolis. The Islanders played their final Hawai'i game in August 1987, then opened the 1988 season as the Colorado Springs Sky Sox.

THE DAY A LOCAL AMATEUR TEAM ALMOST BEAT THE DODGERS.

After being swept by the Baltimore Orioles in the 1966 World Series, the Los Angeles Dodgers stopped in Honolulu en route to Tokyo to play exhibition games against Japanese major league teams. The Dodgers had also agreed to play an exhibition game at Honolulu Stadium against a pickup team of local ballplayers. It should have been no contest, but pitching for the locals was Bo Belinsky, who had once pitched a no-hitter for the California Angels and had been playing for the Hawaii Islanders. In the end the hometown team lost the game, but Belinsky shut out the Dodgers for the first five innings.

The art of deception

In the days before satellite broadcasting, resourceful Hawaii Islanders announcers perfected the fine art of radio recreation. Due to time zone differences, the team's road games were played earlier in the day. So the legendary sportscaster Les Keiter and his colleagues faithfully re-created them for local listeners in prime time, complete with sound effects like the roar of the crowd and the crack of the bat. Many listeners were convinced they were listening to live games.

A MAUI BALLPLAYER HITS THE BIG TIME.

While quite a few local boys have distinguished themselves in Major League Baseball, Maui-born Shane Victorino played 12 seasons for five teams, primarily the Philadelphia Phillies and the Boston Red Sox. Nicknamed the Flyin' Hawaiian, Victorino appeared in two All-Star games and two World Series, one each with the Phillies and the Red Sox. In 2018 his father, Mike, was elected mayor of Maui.

HAWAI'I'S UNCANNY ABILITY TO PRODUCE BIG LEAGUE SPORTSCASTERS.

Most of the announcers hired as the play-by-play voice of the Hawaii Islanders went on to work in a similar capacity in network sports or for major league teams. Harry Kalas, the Islanders' very first play-by-play announcer, was the voice of the Philadelphia Phillies for 38 years and voted into the Baseball Hall of Fame. Al Michaels, who called Islanders games from 1968 to 1970, went on to media stardom announcing for the Cincinnati Reds, Monday Night Football and the Olympics, including his unforgettable exultation in the closing seconds of the US hockey victory over Russia in the 1980 Winter Olympics: *"Do you believe in miracles? Yes!"* Also: Matt Pinto, Mel Proctor, Hank Greenwald, Ken Wilson, Neil Everett and Larry Beil.

Photo Credits

Arthur Suehiro, *Honolulu Stadium: Where Hawaii Played*, 113

David Croxford, 62

Eddie Sherman Collection, 58

Hawai'i State Archives, 48, 75

iStock, 8, 15, 20, 24, 32, 40, 50, 71, 72, 80, 88, 91, 92, 95, 100-02, 107, 116

Panini Productions, 65

©Polynesian Voyaging Society (used with permission), 46-47

University of Hawai'i Archives, 22, 37